Making Graphs

Pictographs

by Vijaya Khisty Bodach

Capstone
press

Mankato, Minnesota

A+ Books are published by Capstone Press,
151 Good Counsel Drive, P.O. Box 669, Mankato, Minnesota 56002.
www.capstonepress.com

1 2 3 4 5 6 12 11 10 09 08 07

Library of Congress Cataloging-in-Publication Data
Bodach, Vijaya.
  Pictographs / by Vijaya Khisty Bodach.
    p. cm.— (A+ books. Making graphs)
  Includes bibliographical references and index.
  ISBN-13: 978-1-4296-0041-5 (hardcover)
  ISBN-10: 1-4296-0041-1 (hardcover)
  1. Mathematics—Charts, diagrams, etc.—Juvenile literature. 2. Graphic methods—Study and
teaching (Elementary)—Juvenile literature. 3. Mathematical statistics—Study and teaching
(Elementary)—Juvenile literature. 4. Signs and symbols—Juvenile literature. 5. Games in
mathematics education—Juvenile litrature. I.Title. II. Series.
  QA90.B62 2008
  001.4'226–dc22   2007006948

Credits
Heather Adamson, editor; Juliette Peters, designer; Wanda Winch, photo researcher;
    Kelly Garvin, photo stylist

Photo Credits
All photos Capstone Press/Karon Dubke except page 10 (bottom) Getty Images Inc./Stone/
    Daniel Bolser, page 11 Brand X, and page 18 iStockphoto/Andresr.

Note to Parents, Teachers, and Librarians
Making Graphs uses color photographs and a nonfiction format to introduce readers to graphing
concepts. *Pictographs* is designed to be read aloud to a pre-reader, or to be read independently
by an early reader. Images and activities encourage mathematical thinking in early readers
and listeners. The book encourages further learning by including the following sections: Table
of Contents, Glossary, Read More, Internet Sites, and Index. Early readers may need assistance
using these features.

Table of Contents

Look at all these bunnies!
Do we have more bunnies that are white
or spotted brown?

Let's put the animals in rows.
Then we can compare.

The row of white bunnies is longer.
We have more white bunnies
than spotted bunnies.

Using pictures is easier than using animals.
Pictographs use pictures to show how many.

The pictograph shows we have more white bunnies. The key at the bottom shows each drawing means one animal.

How do most children get to school?

Let's make a pictograph to find out.

We have kids who ride their bikes, walk, and take a bus. Pictures can help us compare.

= one child

Getting to School

The key shows that each picture
stands for one child.
Most children ride the bus to school.

Now let's make each picture stand
for two children. We change the key.
Then we draw half as many pictures.

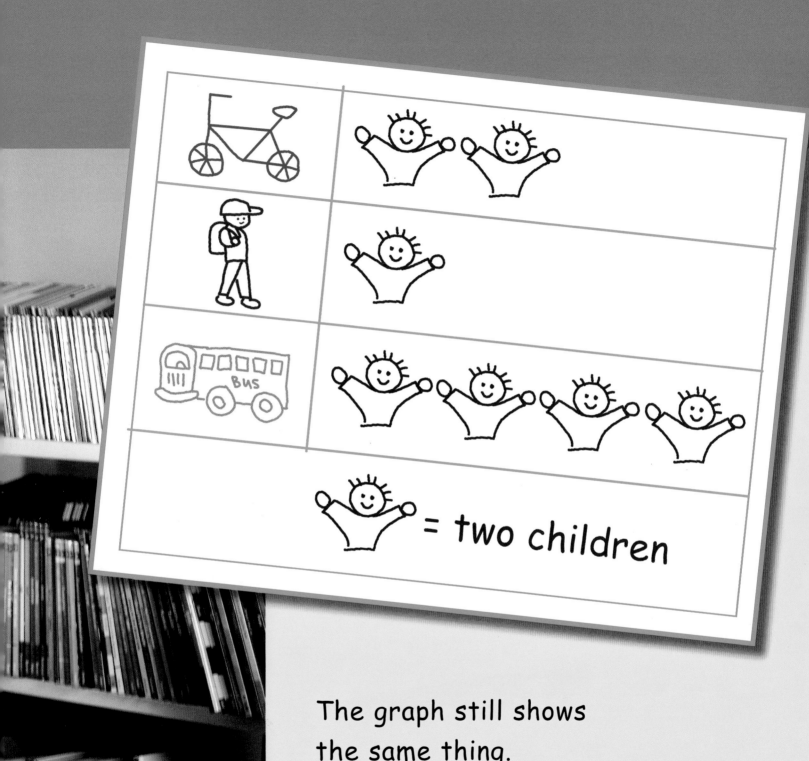

= two children

The graph still shows
the same thing.
Most children ride the bus.

Let's use a pictograph to plan a garden.

My Garden

1 picture = 2 seeds planted

Each picture stands for two seeds planted.
There is room for all our favorites!

A pictograph can show
how well our sunflowers grew.
Not all the seeds sprouted.

We planted ten seeds. Only six plants grew.
We planted more seeds than grew into plants.

seeds   flowers

𝟘 =1   🌼 =1

A pretty bunch of flowers! A pictograph
can show how many flowers of each kind.

This pictograph shows yellow flowers are most popular in this bunch.
There are the fewest white flowers.

1 picture = 1 flower

We are getting ready for a big party.
Let's make a pictograph
of the party supplies.

Party Supplies

balloons   plates   napkins   candles

1 picture = 5

Each picture stands for five items.
We need lots of balloons
but only a few candles.

Milk, juice, or soda pop?
Which party drink will kids choose?

favorite drink

1 picture = 2 drinks
1/2 picture = 1 drink

Juice was the most popular choice.
Fewer kids drank soda or milk.

The pictograph shows that more kids are wearing hats than are blowing noise makers.

What kinds of food do you eat most? Fruits and vegetables? Grains? Dairy or sweets? Make a pictograph and compare.

How does your eating change when you are
in school, home on weekends, or on vacation?

Glossary

compare (kuhm-PARE)—to judge one thing against another

graph (GRAF)—a picture that compares numbers or amounts; graphs use bars, lines, or parts of circles to compare.

key (KEE)—a list or chart that explains symbols on a graph

popular (POP-yuh-lur)—most liked or used most often

row (ROH)—a line of things arranged side by side

Read More

Nechaev, Michelle Wagner. *Making Graphs.* I Can Do Math. Milwaukee: Gareth Stevens Publishing, 2004.

Trumbauer, Lisa. *Graph It!* Math. Mankato, Minn.: Yellow Umbrella Books, 2002.

Internet Sites

FactHound offers a safe, fun way to find Internet sites related to this book. All of the sites on FactHound have been researched by our staff.

Here's how:

1. Visit *www.facthound.com*

2. Choose your grade level.

3. Type in this book ID for **1429600411** age-appropriate sites. You may also browse subjects by clicking on letters, or by clicking on pictures and words.

4. Click on the **Fetch It** button.

FactHound will fetch the best sites for you!

Index